Sacred Heart of Jesus

Saint Alphonsus Liguori
Edited by Thomas M. Santa, C.SS.R.

Liguori

ONE LIGUORI DRIVE
LIGUORI MO 63057-9999
314.464.2500

Imprimi Potest:
Richard Thibodeau, C.SS.R.
Provincial, Denver Province
The Redemptorists

Imprimatur:
+ Paul A. Zipfel, V.G.
Auxiliary Bishop, Archdiocese of St. Louis

The meditations that follow appear in the ascetical works of Saint Alphonsus Liguori, collected and translated from the Italian by Eugene Grimm, C.SS.R. The meditations can be found in volume six, *The Holy Eucharist*, under the title, *Novena to the Sacred Heart of Jesus*. This new edition has been edited and excerpted for private prayer and devotion.

Scripture quotations are taken from *The Christian Community Bible*, Catholic Pastoral Edition, copyright © 1995 by Liguori Publications. All rights reserved.

Cover design by Grady Gunter

Novena to the Sacred Heart of Jesus

Saint Alphonsus Liguori
Edited by Thomas M. Santa, C.SS.R.

A Brief History of the Devotion

Devotion to the Sacred Heart of Jesus is a devotion that focuses attention on the physical heart of Jesus as the symbol of his redemptive love. Although tradition often situates the beginning of the practice of the devotion to the year 1000, it might be more accurate to place its birth during the time of the great mystics (Saint Anselm and Saint Bernard) between 1050 and 1150. By the middle ages, because of a strong emphasis on the passion of our Lord, and because of the efforts of Saint Bonaventure and Saint Gertrude the Great, the devotion became popularized as a means of worshiping the mystery of Christ, living in the Church.

This devotion was promoted by great saints, including Saint Albert the Great, Saint Catherine of Siena, Saint Francis de Sales, as well as great religious orders, such as the Benedictines, the Dominicans, and the Carthusians. However, it must be recorded that the saint who is most often associated with this devotion is Saint Margaret Mary Alacoque (1647-1690). Her private revelations promoted the establishment of a liturgical feast day and the practice of offering reparation for the outrages committed against the Blessed Sacrament. Saint Alphonsus was heavily influenced by Saint Margaret Mary in his own devotion to the Sacred Heart.

In modern times it was Pope Pius IX who, in 1856, established the feast of the Sacred Heart and encouraged the efforts of the Apostleship of Prayer—a confraternity of believers who encouraged groups, families, and communities to consecrate themselves to the Sacred Heart. In 1928 Pope Pius XI issued his encyclical

Miserentissimus Redemptor on reparation to the Sacred Heart. In 1956 Pope Pius XII published his encyclical *Haurietis aquas* on the nature of devotion to the Sacred Heart.

The devotion is usually practiced in preparation for the feast of the Sacred Heart which is celebrated on the Friday following the second Sunday after Pentecost. It is also practiced in conjunction with the monthly *First Friday* observance that is traditional in many families and parishes.

—the editor

Introduction

The devotion of all devotions is love for Jesus Christ.

A devout author laments the sight of so many persons who pay attention to various devotions, but neglect devotion to the Sacred Heart of Jesus. There are many preachers and confessors who say great things, but speak little of love for Jesus Christ.

The love of Jesus Christ ought to be the principal, indeed the only devotion of a Christian. The love of Jesus Christ should be the only object and care of preachers and confessors—all should constantly inflame their listeners' hearts with the love of Jesus Christ. To not do so is the reason why people make so little progress in virtue and remain groveling in the same defects. Lack of devotion to the Sacred Heart is the reason for frequent relapses into serious sin, because people pay scant attention, and are not sufficiently encouraged to acquire the love of Jesus Christ, which is the golden cord which unites and binds the soul to God.

For this reason the Eternal Word came into this world, to make himself loved: *I have come to bring fire upon the earth* (Luke 12:49). For this reason the Eternal Father sent his son into the world, in order that he might make known to us his love, and thus obtain our love in return. The Father will love us in the same proportion as we love Jesus Christ: *For the Father himself loves you because you have loved me and you believe that I came from the Father* (John 16:27). In addition, he gives us graces when we ask in the name of his son: *Whatever you ask the Father in my Name, he will give to you* (John 16:23). However, we will never be formed in the image of the Lord, nor even desire to be formed in his image, if we do not meditate upon the love which Jesus Christ has shown us.

For this purpose it is related in the life of Saint Margaret Mary Alacoque, a nun of the Order of the Visitation, that our Savior revealed to this servant his wish that the devotion and the feast of his Sacred Heart should be established and propagated in the Church. In this way, devout believers would, by their adoration and prayer, make reparation for the injuries his heart constantly receives from ungrateful humanity when he is exposed in the Blessed Sacrament of the altar. It is also related that while this devout sister was praying before the Blessed Sacrament, Jesus Christ showed her his heart surrounded by thorns, with a cross on the top, and in a throne of flames. "Behold the heart," she reports that Jesus spoke to her, "that has loved humanity, and has spared nothing for them, even to consuming itself to give them pledges of its love, but which receives from the majority of people, no other return but ingratitude, and insults toward the sacrament of love."

The devotion to the Sacred Heart of Jesus, is nothing more than an exercise of love toward our loving Savior. Therefore the principal object of this devotion, the spiritual object of this devotion, is the love with which the heart of Jesus is inflamed toward all.

Let us now attempt to satisfy the devotion of those who are enamored of Jesus Christ, and who desire to honor him in the most Holy Sacrament, by a novena of holy meditations and affections to his Sacred Heart.

FIRST MEDITATION
The Amiable Heart of Jesus

The persons who show themselves amiable in all things must be truly loved. If only we dedicated ourselves to discovering all the good qualities by which Jesus Christ makes himself worthy of our love, we would all be required to love him. What heart can be found more worthy of love than the heart of Jesus? A heart all pure, all holy, all full of love toward God and toward us; because all his desires are only for the divine glory and our good. This is the heart in which God finds all his delight. Every perfection and every virtue reign in this heart.

In Jesus is found everything that is appealing and agreeable. Some are attracted to love others by their beauty, others by their innocence, others by living with them, others by devotion. But if there were a person in whom all these and other virtues were united, who would not love them? If we heard that there was in a distant country a foreign prince who was handsome, humble, courteous, devout, full of charity, and who returned good to those who did him evil, then, although we were not acquainted with him, nor was there any possibility of our ever being acquainted, yet we could become enamored with him, and could be required to love him. How is it possible that Jesus Christ, who possesses in himself all these virtues, and in the most perfect degree, and who loves us so tenderly, how is it possible that he is not loved by humanity, and not the only object of our love?

O my God, how is it that Jesus, who alone is worthy of love, and who has given us so many proofs of the love that he has for us, cannot succeed in making us love him! This is what caused floods of tears for Saint Rose of Lima, Saint Catherine of Genoa, Saint Teresa, Saint Mary Magdalen of Pazzi, who, on considering the ingratitude of humanity, exclaimed weeping: "Love is not loved. Love is not loved."

Affections and Prayers

O my amiable Redeemer, who could I love more than you? You are the beauty of paradise, you are the love of your Father, your heart is the throne of virtue. O amiable heart of my Jesus, you deserve the love of all hearts; poor and wretched are the hearts that do not love you. My heart has been miserable, O my God, during all the time that I have not loved you. But I will not continue to be wretched. I love you, I will always continue to love you.

O my Jesus, I have sometimes forgotten you, and now what can I expect? Will my ingratitude force you to forget me and abandon me? No, my Savior, do not permit this. You are the object of the love of God and so you must be loved by a miserable sinner. O lovely flames that burn in the loving heart of my Jesus, enkindle in my poor heart that holy fire which Jesus came down from heaven to light on the earth. Consume and destroy all the impure affections that dwell in my heart and prevent it from being entirely yours.

O my God, grant that my heart may only exist to love you, and you alone, my dearest Savior. If at one time I despised you, you are now the only object of my love. I love you, I love you, I love you, and I will never love anyone else but you. My beloved Lord, do not refuse to accept the love of a heart which has once afflicted you by my sins. Let it be your glory to exhibit to the angels a heart now burning with love for you; a heart which at one time shunned and despised you.

Most holy virgin Mary, my hope. Please assist me, and beg Jesus to make me, by his grace, all that he wishes me to be.

SECOND MEDITATION
The Loving Heart of Jesus

If we could only understand the love that burns in the heart of Jesus for us! He has loved us so much that even if all the people, all the angels, and all the saints were to unite, with all their energies, they could not arrive at the thousandth part of the love that Jesus has for us. He loves us infinitely more that we love ourselves.

Jesus has loved us to excess, and what greater excess of love could there be than for God to die for his creatures? He has loved us to the greatest degree: *As he had loved those who were his own in the world, he would love them with perfect love* (John 13:1). He has loved us from eternity, for there never was a moment from eternity when God did not think of us and did not love each one of us: *I have loved you with an everlasting love* (Jeremiah 31:3). For our love he made himself human and chose a life of suffering and death on the cross for our sake. He has loved us completely and has sacrificed everything to show us the love that he has for us. Isn't this excess of love sufficient to stupefy with astonishment the angels of paradise for all eternity?

This love has also induced him to remain with us in the Holy Sacrament as on a throne of love, for he remains there under the appearance of a small piece of bread, shut up in a ciborium, where he remains in order to love us. Love makes us desire the constant presence of the object of our love. It is this love and this desire that makes Jesus Christ reside with us in the Most Holy Sacrament. The thirty-three years that he spent with us on earth were not long enough. Therefore, in order to demonstrate his desire for being with us, he performed the greatest of all miracles by the institution of the holy Eucharist. He remains there because he cannot separate himself from us.

His love has induced him to become food for our souls, in order to unite himself to us, and make his heart and ours as one: *He who eats my flesh and drinks my blood, lives in me and I in him* (John 6:56). O excess of divine love! This is a mystery of faith above my comprehension; it cannot be understood. O love of Jesus, make yourself known to me and make yourself loved!

Affections and Prayers

O adorable heart of my Jesus, heart inflamed with the love of humanity, heart created on purpose to love them, how is it possible that you can be despised and your love not communicated to humankind? O, miserable that I am, I also have been one of those ungrateful ones that have not loved you. Forgive me, my Jesus, this great sin of not loving you. I feel that I deserve to be condemned to a life of not being able to love you because I have once renounced your love. My Savior, give me any other chastisement but do not inflict this one upon me. Grant me the grace to love you, and then give me any affliction you desire.

O love of my Jesus, you are my love. O burning heart of my Jesus, inflame my heart also. Do not permit me in the future, even for a single moment, to live without your love. I trust in the blood that you have shed for me that I will always love you, and that you will always love me, and that this love between you and me will not be broken off for eternity.

O Mary, Mother of fair love, you who desire so much to see Jesus loved, bind me, unite me to your son, but bind me to him so that we may never again be separated.

THIRD MEDITATION
The Heart of Jesus Christ
Desires to Be Loved

Jesus has no need of us. He is equally happy, equally rich, equally powerful with or without our love. However, as Saint Thomas teaches, he loves us so much that he desires our love as if humanity was his God, and his life depended on humanity. This filled holy Job with astonishment: *What is man that you make much of him, that you give him so much attention?* (Job 7:17).

What? Can God desire or ask with such eagerness for the love of a worm? It would have been a great favor if God had only permitted us to love him. The princes of this earth do not humble themselves to this, but

Jesus, who is the king of heaven, demands our love: *Love the Lord, your God, with all your heart* (Matthew 22:37). So urgently does he ask for our heart: *My [child], give me your heart* (Proverbs 23:26). If he is driven from a soul he does not depart, but he stands outside of the door of the heart, and he calls and knocks to be admitted: *I stand at the door and knock* (Revelation 3:20). In short, Jesus takes delight in being loved by us and is consoled when a person says to him, and repeats often, "My God, my God, I love you."

"Why does God love, but that he might be loved himself," said Saint Bernard, and God himself said, *Love [me] and serve [me] with all your heart and your soul* (Deuteronomy 10:12). Jesus tells us that he is the shepherd, who, having lost his sheep, calls all the others to rejoice with him, *Celebrate with me for I have found my lost sheep* (Luke 15:6). He tells us that he is that Father who, when his lost son returns and throws himself at his feet, not only forgives him, but embraces him tenderly. Can we not be moved to respond to God's love by such invitations and promises?

Affections and Prayers

My dearest Redeemer, I will say to you, with Saint Augustine, that you command me to love you and you threaten me with hell if I do not love you. What can be more dreadful than hell? What greater misfortune can happen than to be deprived of your love? If you desire to frighten me, threaten me only that I should have to continue living without loving you—for this threat alone will frighten me more than a thousand hells. If, in the midst of the flames of hell, the damned could burn with your love, O my God, then hell itself would become a paradise. If, on the contrary, the blessed in heaven could not love you, then paradise would become hell. This is what Saint Augustine is trying to teach us.

I see indeed, my dearest lord, that on account of my sins I deserve to be abandoned by your grace. At the same time I deserve to be condemned to be incapable of loving you, but I still understand that you continue to command me to love you, and I also feel within me a great desire to love you. This desire is a gift of your grace, and it comes from you. Give me the strength necessary to put your grace into action, and make me, from this day forward, a person who can pray from the bottom of my heart, and to repeat to you always, "My God, I love you, I love you, I love you!" Blot out from your memory the sins that I have committed against you. Let us love each other from this day forward. I will not leave you, and you will not leave me. You will always love me, and I will always love you.

O Mary, Immaculate Virgin, please help me and please petition Jesus for me.

FOURTH MEDITATION
The Sorrowful Heart of Jesus

It is impossible to consider how afflicted the heart of Jesus is for our love and not pity him. He tells us that his heart is overwhelmed with sorrow: *My soul is full of sorrow, even to death* (Mark 14:34). The principle sorrow which afflicted his heart is not the sight of the torments and infamy which humankind prepared for him, but rather the sight of their ingratitude toward his immense love. Jesus foresaw all of the sins which we would commit after all of his sufferings and after such a bitter and ignominious death. He foresaw the horrible insults which people would offer to his adorable heart which he has left us in the Most Holy Sacrament as a proof of his love. O my God, what insults has Jesus received in this sacrament of love!

And yet, the sight of all of these insults did not prevent him from leaving us this great pledge of his love. He hates sin, still it seems as if his love toward us had overcome the hatred he feels for sin, since he was resigned to permit these sacrileges, rather than deprive the souls that love him of this divine food. Shouldn't this make us love a heart that has loved us so much?

Jesus Christ has done enough to deserve our love. Ungrateful that we are, shall we still leave Jesus abandoned on the altar, as the majority of people do? Should we not unite ourselves to those few people who acknowledge him? The heart of Jesus remains in the sacrament, burning with love for us. Should we not, in his presence, burn with love for Jesus?

Affections and Prayers

My adorable and dearest Jesus, behold at your feet a person who has caused so much sorrow to your amiable heart. O my God, how could I wound your heart, which has loved me so much, and has spared nothing to make itself loved by me? But console yourself, I will say to my savior, for my heart, having been wounded with your grace and most holy love, now feels regret for the offenses that I have committed against you. Please give me, my Jesus, the sorrow for my sins which you felt for them in your life! Eternal Father, I offer you the sorrow your son felt for my sins. I ask you to give me a great sorrow for the offenses I have committed against you so that I may live a life that no longer despises your friendship.

My Lord Jesus, from this day forward, give me a horror of sin, that I may despise even the slightest faults, considering that they displease you. My beloved Lord, I now detest everything that displeases you, and in the future I will love only you, and love only that which you love. Oh help me, give me the strength, give me the grace to call upon you constantly, O my Jesus, and always to repeat to you this petition: My Jesus, give me your love, give me your love, give me your love.

Most holy Mary, obtain for me the grace to pray to you continually and to say to you, O my Mother, make me love Jesus Christ.

FIFTH MEDITATION
The Compassionate Heart of Jesus

Where shall we ever find a heart that is more compassionate or tender or had a greater empathy for our misery than the heart of Jesus?

This compassion induced Jesus to descend from heaven to this earth. It made him say that he was that good shepherd who came to give his life to save his sheep. In order to obtain pardon for our sins, he would not spare himself, but would sacrifice himself on the cross. By his sufferings he has substituted himself for the chastisement that we deserve. This pity and compassion makes him say even now: *Why should you die, Israel? I do not want the death of anyone,...but that you be converted and live!* (Ezekiel 18:31-32). My poor children, why will you damn yourselves by fleeing from me? Do you not see that by separating yourselves from me you are hastening to eternal death? I do not desire to see you lost. Do not despair. As often as you wish to return, return, and you shall recover your life. *Be converted, and live!*

O my Jesus, you pardon the repentant

sinner, and you give them everything in Holy Communion during their life. Even in heaven, with eternal glory, you do not demonstrate the slightest repugnance being united with a soul that has offended you. Where, then is there to be found a heart so amiable and compassionate as yours, O my dearest Savior?

Affections and Prayers

O compassionate heart of my Jesus, have pity on me: Most sweet Jesus, have mercy on me. I say so now, and beseech you to give me the grace always to say to you, "Most sweet Jesus, have mercy on me." Even before I offended you, O my Redeemer, I certainly did not deserve any of the favors that you have bestowed on me. You have created me, you have given me light and knowledge, and all without any merit of mine. But I have offended you. I not only did not deserve your favor, but I deserve to be abandoned by you and cast into hell. Your compassion has made you wait for me and preserve my life even when I have offended you. Your compassion has enlightened me and offered me pardon. It has given me sorrow for my sins and the desire of loving you, and now I hope for your mercy to always remain in your grace. O my Jesus, do not cease to show your compassion toward me. I love you, and I will always love you. Never permit me to be separated from you; never permit me to be separated from you.

O Mary, my mother, never permit me to be separated from my God.

SIXTH MEDITATION
The Generous Heart of Jesus

It is the characteristic of good-hearted people to desire to make everyone happy, especially those who may be distressed and afflicted. But who can ever find a person who has a better heart than Jesus Christ? He is infinite goodness, and has an overwhelming desire to communicate his riches to his people: *Riches and honor are with me,…*

[which I give] to those who love me (Proverbs 8:18,21). For this reason he made himself poor, as the apostle says, that he might make us rich: *Although he was rich, he made himself poor to make you rich through his poverty* (2 Corinthians 8:9). For this purpose he has also chosen to remain with us in the Most Holy Sacrament, where he remains constantly with his hands full of graces, ready to dispense them to those who come to visit him. For this reason he also gives himself completely to us in holy Communion, helping us to understand from this that he cannot refuse us any good gifts, since he even gives himself entirely to us: *How will he not give us all things with him?* (Romans 8:32).

In the heart of Jesus we receive every good, every grace that we desire: *For you have been fully enriched....You do not lack any spiritual gift* (1 Corinthians 1:5,7). We must understand that we are debtors to the heart of Jesus for all the graces we have received—graces of redemption, of vocation, of light, of pardon; the grace to resist temptations, and to bear patiently with contradictions—for without his assistance we could not do anything good: *Apart from me you can do nothing* (John 15:5).

Our Savior says, if you have not received the graces that you desire, do not complain to me, but blame yourself, because you have neglected to seek them from me: *So far you have not asked in my Name; ask and receive that your joy may be full* (John 16:24). How liberal is the heart of Jesus toward anyone who calls upon him! *All have the same Lord, who is very generous with whoever calls on him* (Romans 10:12). What great mercies do those believers receive who are sincere in asking for Jesus to help them! Let us therefore always go to this heart, and ask with confidence, and we shall obtain what we want.

Affections and Prayers

Ah, my Jesus, you have not refused to give me your blood and your life. Shall I refuse to give you my miserable heart? No, my dearest Redeemer, I offer it entirely to you. I give you all my will. Please accept it and dispose of it at your pleasure. I can do nothing, and have nothing, but I have this heart which you have given to me. I may be deprived of my possessions, my blood, my life, but never my heart. With this heart I can love you; with this heart I will love you. I beseech you, O my God, teach me a perfect forgetfulness of myself. Teach me what I must do in order to acquire your pure love, which in your goodness you have inspired me to desire. I feel in myself a determination to please you, but in order to put my resolve into practice, I expect and implore the necessary help from you. It depends on you, O loving heart of Jesus, to make my heart entirely yours. Grant that my will may be on fire with love for you.

Blessed are you, O Immaculate Virgin Mary, who has always had your heart united to the heart of Jesus. Obtain this for me, O my Mother: that in the future I may wish and desire that which Jesus wills and what you will.

SEVENTH MEDITATION
The Grateful Heart of Jesus

The heart of Jesus is so grateful that it cannot experience even the most insignificant works done for love—our smallest word, a single, good thought—without giving to each its own reward. Jesus is always so grateful that he returns a hundredfold for one: *They will receive a hundredfold and be given eternal life* (Matthew 19:29).

Human beings, when they are grateful, usually return favor for favor. They, as it were, return the obligation and then think no more of it. Jesus Christ does not repeat our example. Rather, he returns a hundredfold in this life for every good action that we perform to please him, and in the next life, returns it in an infinite number of times throughout eternity. Who will be so negligent as not to do as much as possible to please this grateful heart?

O my God, how do people try to please you? Or rather, should I ask, how can people be so ungrateful towards this, our Savior? If he had only shed a single drop of blood, or one tear alone for our salvation, we should still be under infinite obligation to him, because this drop and this tear would have been of infinite value in the sight of God toward obtaining for us every grace. But Jesus has given us all his merits, all his sufferings, all his ignominies, all his blood, and his life, so that we are under, not one, but infinite obligations to love him.

If a little dog shows us any sign of affection it seems to demand us to love it in return. How, then, can we be so ungrateful toward God? It seems as if the benefits of God toward us change our nature: instead of gratitude and love, they obtain nothing but offenses and injuries. O Lord, enlighten ungrateful humankind to know the love that you bear for us.

Affections and Prayers

O my beloved Jesus, behold at your feet an ungrateful sinner. I have been grateful toward creatures, but to you alone I have been ungrateful; to you, who have died for me, and who has done all that you can do to make me love you.

My dearest Jesus, I have often offended you and despised you, but now I love you more than everything, including more than myself! Tell me what you would have me do, for I am ready to do everything with your help. I believe that you have created me. I believe that you have given me your blood and your life so that I may live. I believe that for my sake you remain in the Blessed Sacrament. I thank you for it, O my love. Do not permit me to be ungrateful in the future for the many benefits and proofs of your love. O bind me, unite me to your heart, and permit me never to offend you or grieve you in the years that I have remaining in my life. I have displeased you. Now it is time that I should love you. Oh, that those years that I have lost would return. I know that they will not return, and that the life that remains for me may be short. But regardless of whether it be short or long, I desire to spend it all in loving you, my sovereign good, who deserves an eternal and an infinite love.

O Mary, my Mother, let me never again be ungrateful to your son. Pray to Jesus for me.

EIGHTH MEDITATION
The Despised Heart of Jesus

There is no greater sorrow for a heart that loves than to see its love despised. It is all the more sorrowful when, on the one hand, the proofs given of this love have been great, and, on the other hand, the ingratitude has also been great.

If we were to renounce all our property and if we were to go and live in the desert, to feed on herbs, to sleep on the bare earth, to practice every penance, and at last to give ourselves up to be killed for the sake of Christ, what could we offer in payment for the sufferings, the blood, and the life that this great Son of God has given for our sakes? If we were to sacrifice ourselves every moment till death, we would certainly not make even the slightest downpayment for the love that Jesus Christ has shown us by giving himself to us in the Most Holy Sacrament.

O my God, what payment and grateful thanks does humanity offer to Jesus Christ? Ill treatment, contempt of his laws and his maxims—injuries that they would not inflict on their enemy or the greatest villain on the earth—all of these injuries Jesus has received, and still receives every day. How can we not feel sorrow for them and not at least attempt, by our love, to repay the infinite love of his divine heart, which remains in the Holy Sacrament, inflamed with love for us, and anxious to give us every good gift?

We are accustomed to hearing of the Creation, the Incarnation, Redemption; of Jesus born in a stable and of Jesus dead on the cross. O my God, if we knew that another person had given us any of these benefits, we could not help but love them. It seems that God alone has, so to say, that bad luck with humankind that although he has done all that is possible to make us love him, yet he cannot accomplish this goal. Instead of being loved, God sees himself despised and neglected. All of this comes from forgetfulness of humankind for the love of God.

Affections and Prayers

O heart of Jesus, abyss of mercy and love, how is it that, at the sight of the goodness that you have shown me, and of my ingratitude, that I do not die of sorrow? You, my Savior, after having given me my life, have also given me all your blood and your life by giving yourself up for my sake to suffering and death. Not content with this, you also sacrificed yourself everyday for me in the holy Eucharist. O my God, how can I see myself being so ungrateful to you? O Lord, put an end, I pray, to my ingratitude, by wounding my heart with your love and making me entirely yours. Remember the blood and the tears that you have shed for me, and forgive me. Do not let all of your sufferings be wasted upon me. Even though I have been ungrateful and unworthy of your love you did not cease to love me, even when I did not love you and even when I did not even desire to love you. Grant me today the grace to begin to love you. Make me die to everything in myself in order that I may live only for you and that I may always burn with your love.

O Mary, your heart was the blessed altar that was always on fire with divine love. My dearest Mother, make me like you. Obtain for me this grace from your son, who delights in honoring you, by denying nothing that you ask of him.

NINTH MEDITATION
The Faithful Heart of Jesus

How faithful is the beautiful heart of Jesus towards those whom he calls to his love. *He who called you is faithful and will do it* (1 Thessalonians 5:24).

The faithfulness of God gives us the confidence to hope for all things, even though we deserve nothing. If we have driven God from our heart, let us open the door to God, and he will immediately enter, according to the promise that he has made. *I stand at the door and knock. If anyone hears my call and opens the door, I will come in to him* (Revelation 3:20). If we wish for graces, let us ask for them from God, in the name of Jesus, and he has promised that we will receive them: *Whatever you ask the Father in my Name, he will give you* (John 16:23). If we are tempted, let us trust in his merits, knowing that he will not permit our enemies to challenge us beyond our strength: *God is faithful and will not let you be tempted beyond your strength* (1 Corinthians 10:13).

Contrast the faithfulness of God to the faithfulness of humankind. How often do human beings promise, and then fail, either because they tell lies in making their promises, or because, after having made the promise, they change their minds. *God is not man that he should lie, nor a son of man that he should repent. Has he said he will do something and will not do it? Has he promised something and not fulfilled it?* (Numbers 23:19). God cannot be unfaithful to his promises because, being truth itself, God cannot lie. Also, God cannot change his mind because all that he wills is just and right. God has promised to give help to all who ask and to love all who love him.

If we could only be as faithful to God as God is faithful to us! How often have we, in times past, promised him that we would serve him and love him, only to have then betrayed him, and, renouncing his service, sold ourselves as slaves to the devil. Let us ask the Lord to give us strength to be faithful to God for the future. How blessed will we be if we are faithful to Jesus Christ in the few things that he commands us to do. *Very well, good and faithful servant, since you have been faithful in a few things, I will entrust you with much more. Come and share the joy of your master!* (Matthew 25:21).

Affections and Prayers

If I would only be as faithful to you, my dearest Redeemer, as you have been faithful to me. Whenever I have opened my heart to you, you have entered in, to forgive me and to receive me into your love. Whenever I have called, you have come to my assistance. You have been faithful toward me but I have been exceedingly unfaithful toward you. I have promised you my love and then have many times refused to give it to you as if you, my God, who has created and redeemed me, were less worthy of being loved than one of your creatures or some miserable pleasure. Forgive me, my Jesus. I know my ingratitude and I abhor it. I know that you are infinite goodness and that you deserve infinite love, especially from me, whom you have loved, even after all of the sins that I have committed against you.

O loving and faithful heart of Jesus, inflame my miserable heart so that it will burn for love of you. My Jesus, it seems to me that now I love you, but I love you just a little. Make me love you exceedingly. Make me remain faithful to you until death. I ask you for this grace, together with the grace of always praying to you for even more grace and blessings. Grant that I may die than betray you again.

Mary, my Mother, help me to be faithful to your son.

CONCLUDING PRAYER
TO THE
SACRED HEART OF JESUS

O loving heart of my Redeemer. You are the source of all virtue, the source of all graces, the burning furnace in which all holy people are inflamed with your love. You are the object of God's love, you are the refuge of the afflicted, and the home of all souls who love you.

Your heart was wounded for me on the

cross by the lance of my sins. Your heart remains with me in the Blessed Sacrament of the altar. Your heart loves all people with tenderness, and is loved so little in return. Inflame all hearts with true love for you!

Why can't I travel all over the world to make your graces known, to let all people know of your sweetness and the treasures that you distribute to all who love you? Accept my desire to have all hearts love you. Be my consolation in trials, my rest in work, my comfort in anxiety, my harbor in the storm. I consecrate to you my body and my soul, my heart and my life, together with all that I am. I unite all my thoughts to you, along with my affections and my desires.

O Eternal Father! I offer you the pure affections of the heart of Jesus. If you reject me, you cannot reject your son. May his heart supply to my heart that which is lacking so that I may be made pleasing to you.